IMPROVING
THE RIDER'S POSITION

by

Joni Bentley

Illustrations by

Carole Vincer

KENILWORTH PRESS

First published in Great Britain by
The Kenilworth Press Limited,
Addington, Buckingham, MK18 2JR

© The Kenilworth Press Limited 1995
Reprinted 1996, 1998

British Library Cataloguing in Publication Data
A catalogue record for this book is available from the British Library.

ISBN 1-872082-65-3

Typeset by Kenilworth Press

Printed in Great Britain by Westway Offset, Wembley

CONTENTS ■■■■■■■■■■■■■■■■■■■

Introduction

One of the greatest challenges to the rider is maintaining a good effective position whilst at the same time remaining in balance with the horse as it moves.

Achieving a good riding position will enable you to direct the horse without hindering his natural grace and beauty. Slumping, straining, tightening and forcing will interfere with the horse's natural flow.

Horses are extremely sensitive creatures. They rely on the signals the rider gives throughout his body, for guidance. This can be misleading if the rider has limited knowledge of his own body and how it works. If the rider is using his mind and body well, he will be open to 'feel'. His commands will be reliable. Communication (aids) between horse and rider will be coherent. Full potential will be realised.

As riders, we concentrate heavily on our horse's way of going – but what of ours? We expect our horses to be **calm**, **straight** and **forwards**, at all times – but these qualities could equally apply to the rider:

- **Calm** – centred mind and body working in harmony in the present moment.
- **Straight** – vertically, in the movement; laterally, weight distributed equally over the horse's back. Rider 'equal on both reins!'
- **Forwards** – the head is leading the rider's movement from a relaxed but toned neck and spine using its optimum length and strength to absorb and direct the horse.

The aim of this book is to show how riding with good posture will not only improve your performance in the saddle, but also that of your horse. Moreover, it will have a beneficial effect on your health and everyday life.

What is a good riding position?

Before moving on to a more detailed discussion of how to improve your performance in the saddle, it helps to outline the key elements that go to make a good riding position.

- Ear, shoulder, hip and heel in a vertical line
- Head freely poised on top of the spine
- Shoulders relaxed
- Shoulder blades flat
- Chest round but soft
- Upper arm hanging down vertically
- Distinct bend in the elbow
- Wrists straight
- Straight line through elbow, wrist to horse's mouth
- Weight evenly distributed on seat bones
- Leg hanging down naturally
- Knee relaxed
- Calf *resting* against the horse's side
- Relaxed ankle
- Foot below the rider's seat
- Stirrup iron on the ball of the foot
- Heels lower than toes

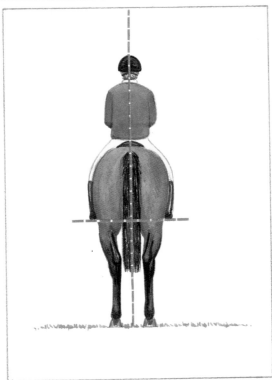

Sitting in the vertical

If our posture is poor, the body cannot work efficiently. In the illustrations opposite you can see how the figure on the left is standing well (in horsey terms, in a good outline or 'on the bit'), whilst the one on the right is slouched (in a poor outline, or 'on the forehand'). This latter posture will eventually lead to stiffness and back problems, and will prevent the rider from being effective.

When sitting on a saddle, in order for your upper body, head, neck and back to be in correct alignment with ease and poise you must sit on the lowest central point of your seat bones. In fact it helps to think of your seat bones as little feet (seat feet) that are supporting the weight of your upper body.

The seat bones are shaped like little rockers with a front, middle and back. To find the lowest central part, sit on your hands, palms up. They may be more

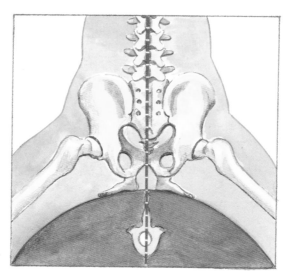

Thinking of your seat bones as 'seat feet' gives more stability to your upper body. Make sure they sit evenly on either side of the horse's spine.

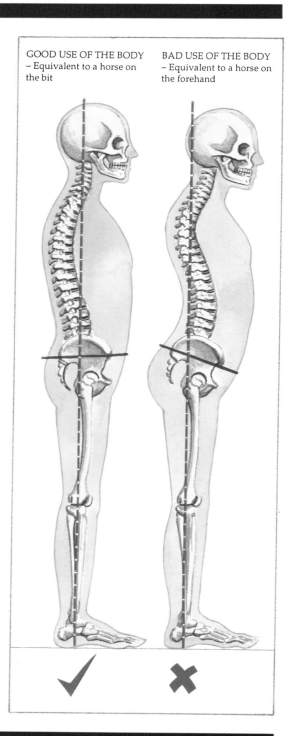

GOOD USE OF THE BODY
– Equivalent to a horse on the bit

BAD USE OF THE BODY
– Equivalent to a horse on the forehand

SITTING ON THE BACK RIM OF THE SEAT BONES	SITTING ON THE FRONT RIM OF THE PELVIS	GOOD VERTICAL ALIGNMENT
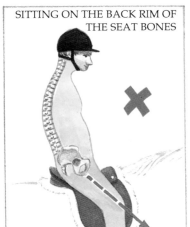		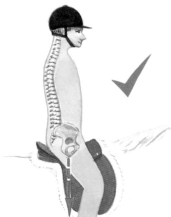
This puts pressure on the whole spine and leaves you behind the movement. It is almost impossible to bring your leg underneath you and maintain correct alignment.	This arches and stiffens your lower back and neck, putting you 'above the bit' and in front of the movement.	Sitting on the lowest, most central part of your seat bones makes vertical alignment easy. Strain and pressure are taken away.
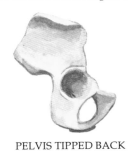	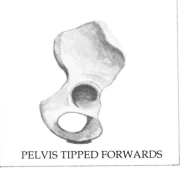	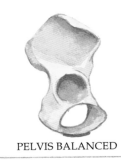
PELVIS TIPPED BACK	PELVIS TIPPED FORWARDS	PELVIS BALANCED

forwards than you imagined. If you have difficulty finding them, rock from one to the other. Now find and balance on the lowest central part of their arc and distribute your weight **evenly** between them. This is the basis of sitting in the vertical.

Rock very slowly backwards along the rim of the seat bones until you find the back edge. You will now be sitting with your pelvis tipped backwards. Notice how it has affected your head, neck, back, chest and shoulders. Do you feel any upward support from the saddle beneath

you or are you pressing down too heavily to sense it?

Come to the vertical again, taking note of the change in your upper body. You should sense that your weight is going downwards but is balanced by the support of the saddle and horse.

Now explore the front edge of the rockers. As you roll forwards you will see that your lower back tends to arch and your ribcage lifts. Rock back to the vertical position then to the front several times and notice how you come up and off your seat bones.

Even weight distribution

It is essential that the weight of the rider is evenly distributed across the horse's back, and that the rider sits evenly on both seat bones. If the rider is crooked (uneven) the horse soon learns to compensate for his uneven load – result: crookedness in the horse.

If, for example, you are naturally right-handed, the right side of your body may be stronger but shorter than the left, displacing the left side laterally. The rider who sits collapsed to the inside tends to push his hips to the outside and often the whole body is twisted.

To help to correct this unevenness stretch your hands into the air, fingertips to the sky, palms facing inwards. Let the accumulated weight of your head, neck, shoulders, arms and upper body pass directly downwards through your torso to the central lowest part of your seat bones, until the weight is even, i.e. laterally and vertically. Notice if you have a tendency to lift your chest. If so, allow it to release down and notice if tension decreases in your lower back.

Ask a friend to give you feedback. The new, correct position will feel unusual for a time.

Experiment also by moving your head around and notice any effect this has on your 'seat feet'.

Now, with fingertips pointing to the sky, practise alternate lengthening very subtly through each side of your torso. Sense your weight changing as it passes down to your seat bones. Keep the balance on the central lowest part. The more you stretch up and allow your ribs to open and stretch, giving them life and space, the more you allow your lower body and 'seat feet' to release down and receive the upward support of the horse.

A crooked man walks a crooked mile. As you are on the ground, so you are on the horse. Becoming aware of your crookedness is the starting point to straightness.

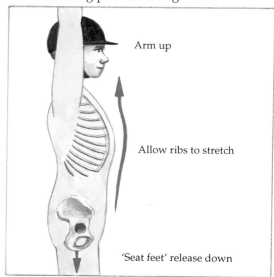

Arm up

Allow ribs to stretch

'Seat feet' release down

Exercise to make the rider equal on both reins. Use this opposing stretch – hand up, 'seat foot' down – to give more freedom and suppleness to the ribcage.

Head and neck

The way the rider's head is balanced on top of the spine determines how well the body will be able to take up a good riding position. If the head is not poised correctly, the back will not be able to absorb the horse's movement.

If you jam your jaw into your neck, notice how this restricts the freedom of your head, neck and back (just like a horse behind the bit). Many riders mistakenly think that pulling in a horse's head in the same way puts him on the bit. Unfortunately what they are doing (as you can feel in yourself) is restricting the elasticity and tone of his head, neck and back.

If you pull your head back and down, notice the strain and downwards pressure on your back – very uncomfortable, just as it is in your horse when he goes above the bit.

For the rider to be 'on the bit', slightly flex forwards between the ears and behind the nose.

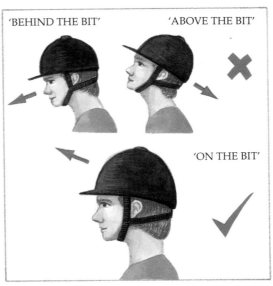

With a delicate forward flexion from the mid-point between the ears and the nose, allow your head to ease forwards and up, without tightening your neck.

The legs and feet

The action of the legs and feet are vitally important and sadly neglected in training, especially from the knee down. In order for your ankles and knees to act as springs and shock-absorbers first you need to be able to release (relax) them. Release the front of the ankle and continue that release up to the knee cap. Then release the back of the knee and allow that release to continue down into the calf muscle to the back of the ankle through the heel bone and down to the floor. This allows the heel to drop – a vital ingredient for an effective, stable position and creating impulsion (oomph) behind your riding.

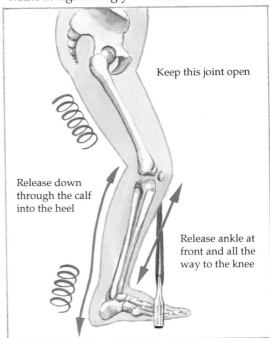

The rider's attention

The very least you can give your horse while training is your undivided attention. To do this you need to be conscious of how your mind works. The mind has a tendency to constantly travel between past, present and future, e.g. if your mind is filled with negative memories from the past, or fears of what could happen in the future, you are living in a permanent state of tension – and losing sight of what is happening to you right now! As the past has gone and you have no control over the future, it is a pretty useless waste of energy and valuable learning time.

And, of course, if the rider is tense, this transmits itself to the horse via minute physiological signals. Sometimes the horse reacts with fear too (by spooking, for instance), which makes the rider even more tense.

Just for a minute, stop reading and take your attention to your body, especially your breathing. Notice how this quietens the mind. It slows the supply of stress hormones to the body and allows the body to relax and clear itself of accumulated tension.

'Time travelling' has an effect of dulling and closing down the mind, like tunnel vision. When you notice this happening, in order to help your mind open up again, look around at your surroundings. Listen to the sounds around you or click your fingers. This will help you to open up again to the present moment.

Fear causes the mind to play tricks. You can see this often in people who are frightened of jumping. The mind loses its sense of reality and projects blindly into the future, seeing problems before they occur, rendering the rider ineffective and fulfilling the prophecy. If you find this happening to you, take your attention to your breathing. Look over and beyond the jump, be aware of your whole surroundings. Now the jump will look smaller and less threatening.

This rider is remembering her holiday, and is therefore not concentrating fully on guiding her horse. With polework and jumping this can lead to injury.

This rider is approaching the jump fearful of what might happen. This panicking can actually cause a fall.

Rein contact

Finding the right rein contact seems to be something of a tricky problem for most riders. Here are a few ideas to help you have a good conversation with your horse's mouth.

Let the horse move your hands through the reins and have the idea that your hands are 'thinking forwards' towards the horse's mouth, not backwards towards your hips. This thinking forwards encourages the horse continually to lengthen his spine and go forwards into the bit. The more he is free in his head, neck and back, the more efficient his breathing becomes and the more effortlessly he can produce the school movements you require of him.

Allow your hands to follow the backwards and forwards movement of the horse's head, so his neck can be long and flowing rather than tight and restricted. With this light contact, sense the fleshy sides of the horse's mouth through the reins. After a short time, if you don't hassle him, he will start to take the bit forwards and away from you. This is the first stage of working on the bit and a prerequisite for straightness.

To help develop a sensitive feel in your hands imagine that you are holding two little birds (as shown). You want to carry them gently but securely; you certainly wouldn't want to crush them to death.

Check your own position frequently: see that your neck is free, your shoulders are relaxed and elbows are relaxed and dropping down. Allow your elbows to lie slightly out away from your ribcage without fixing them. Think of the insides of your wrists as having beams of light shining towards each other. This will help keep your hands in the correct position: palms relaxed, fingertip pads resting on the inside of your palms.

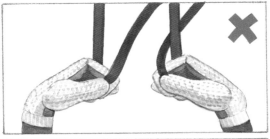
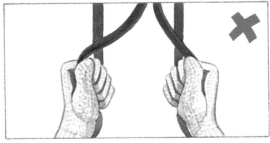

Tension in the hands locks the arms. As a result the horse may stiffen his jaw to avoid the discomfort.

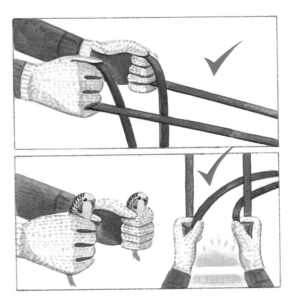

Imagine you are holding two little birds – don't crush them, or allow them to escape. Think also of a beam of light joining the wrists together.

Seeking the contact

1. Initially ride in walk on a free rein and watch where the horse wants to put his head. Notice how the head moves forward and back.

2. Lean forward and stroke both sides of the neck. Then stroke the right side as you take up a contact on the left rein. If the horse is not taking the bit forward he will shorten his neck.

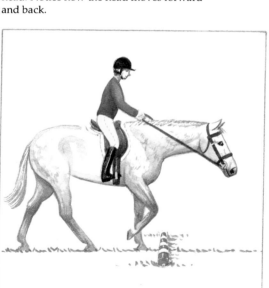

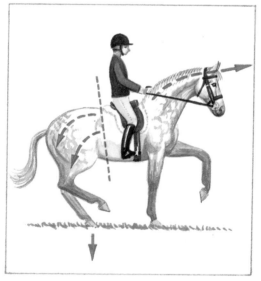

Don't worry if he lengthens the underside of his neck as he stretches more into your hands (*above left*). In order to ultimately achieve collection (*above right*) your horse must be able to stretch the whole of his spine. The more he stretches, the more he strengthens his whole frame, needed for more advanced work

3. Take a contact with the right rein and stroke the left side of the neck. The horse should still take the bit forwards.

4. Now you have taken up the slack, allow the horse to put his head where he wants to. Follow him sensitively and he will start to take the bit forwards into your hands.

CHECK YOUR OWN POSITION FREQUENTLY

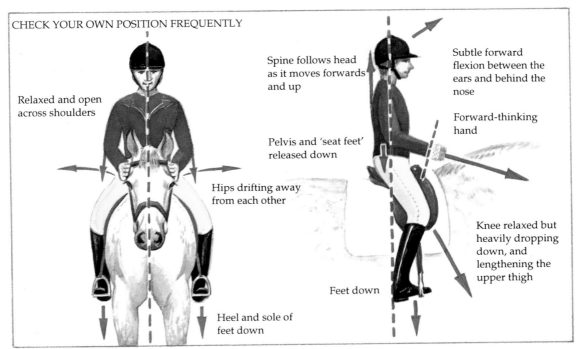

Relaxed and open across shoulders

Spine follows head as it moves forwards and up

Pelvis and 'seat feet' released down

Hips drifting away from each other

Heel and sole of feet down

Subtle forward flexion between the ears and behind the nose

Forward-thinking hand

Knee relaxed but heavily dropping down, and lengthening the upper thigh

Feet down

Bareback work

Riding bareback creates a sensitive rapport between horse and rider, and helps you to better understand how your horse's body works. Before you attempt this work, though, make sure that you have a suitable (quiet) horse and a friend to lead you in a safe area.

Anatomically your skeletal structure predisposes you to ride: the division of your torso at the waist separates your ribcage from your pelvis, giving you the flexibility to absorb the horse's movement. You can carry your upper body while giving your lower back/pelvis to the horse.

First, check that you are not sitting with too much tension, lifting yourself up off the horse's back, or with too little, pressing heavily down into his back. Allow the weight of your head, neck and back to release down onto your seat bones.

Ask a friend to lead you; stay in walk on a loose rein. Sense the horse's spine moving under your 'seat feet' and check that they are evenly supporting the weight above them. Because you are used to your own crookedness, moving into straightness often feels wrong. Knowing this, be prepared to experiment and ask a friend for feedback.

Now lift your arms up into the air. Stretch up through your fingertips to the sky, palms inwards, and rotate your little fingers inwards slightly. Allow your whole body (excluding head) to 'hang' from your fingertips. Your 'seat feet' on either side of the horse's spine can now release even more into the upwards support of the horse's back. Feel the movement of the horse under you. Now lower your arms without collapsing your ribcage.

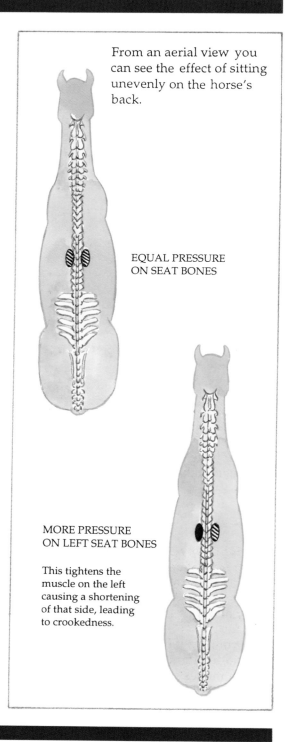

From an aerial view you can see the effect of sitting unevenly on the horse's back.

EQUAL PRESSURE ON SEAT BONES

MORE PRESSURE ON LEFT SEAT BONES

This tightens the muscle on the left causing a shortening of that side, leading to crookedness.

When you ride along feel the horse's ribcage swing from side to side as he brings one hind leg under then the other. Notice that as his ribcage swings to the right, your left seat foot and leg drop down. Let that side of your ribcage be fuller and over the dropping seat bone and leg without collapsing the other side of your ribcage.

Practise the following exercise until you can feel your hips move in all directions – up, down, back, forwards, out to the side.

Exercise to create a deep and supple seat
Ride in walk with your friend leading, and ask him/her to read out the questions below (take two minutes for each question). To help deepen your sensitivity, close your eyes (safety permitting):
• Can you feel the horse move your left hip and seat bone:
(1) upwards? .
(2) downwards?
(3) forwards?
(4) backwards?
(5) sideways?

If you have difficulty with the sideways movement, take your attention to the horse's swinging ribcage.
• Now do the same with the right hip and seat bone.

Exercise to develop straightness
Put your right arm in the air, fingertips pointing to the sky. As you feel the horse's ribcage swing over to the left, subtly allow your right seat bone to drop even further down while, at the same time, your right fingertips reach up to the sky and the right-hand side of your ribcage moves a little to the right. Feel how this stretches the muscles in between the ribs. Repeat with the left arm.

As the horse's ribcage moves to the left, the rider's right seat bone and leg drop down to the floor. The opposite applies as his ribcage moves to the right.

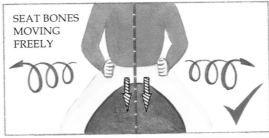

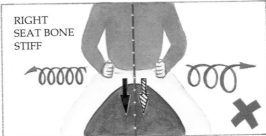

The lower rider's right seat bone is stiff and will lock the horse's back on the right side.

Walk

The walk is a four-beat gait. At all times the horse has three feet on the ground, his body never being in suspension. The saddle is thus tipped around more than at any other gait.

Your balance and ease of movement, as with all paces, greatly affects the horse at walk. A good walk should have a natural long-swinging stride. If you are rough in your riding (pushing with your seat or over-dominating) the horse will tighten up his frame to protect himself and trudge slowly with shorter steps (some riders mistake this as laziness).

Horses are often forced into shapes like this, the effect of which is to lock up the head, neck and back mechanism. This produces stilted paces, discomfort in the horse, and limits his potential.

Improving 'feel' will help you to recognise the symptoms of tightening in the horse. Tension in the horse is often caused by tension in the rider. So to break the spiral, first check your own 'way of going'. To help you relax more, take time to feel the upward support of your horse's back through your whole body.

Developing a good position whilst in motion

Most untrained riders sit as if in a chair, with the legs in front of the vertical. Unfortunately this puts the rider behind the movement. To help them to come more underneath you – putting you more into the movement with the horse – complete the exercise shown opposite, first at walk. As you lie on the horse, relax your neck and pelvis. Stay there until you completely let go. Ask a friend to lead the horse at walk and feel all the different movements.

WALK EXERCISE TO IMPROVE LEG POSITION

Lie on your horse like a floppy doll.

'Walk' your knees back, then push yourself up to vertical with your hands.

You will be surprised how far back your lower leg has to go in order for your knee to point vertically to the ground.

When your upper leg is more supple and vertical, direct the heels and soles of your feet to the ground, as though you are standing with a horse in between your legs.

The illustrations on this page are designed to help you to sit up straight without strain or tension. If you sit up by lifting your chest (like a sergeant major), this will immediately hollow your lower back, which prevents you from absorbing the horse's movement.

If you have a tendency to raise your chest like this you can use the directions in the caption below to help it rest in a more comfortable, natural postition while still maintaining good poise. On the other hand, if you have a tendency to slouch and look down, the directions will help you to open the front of your body, correcting the collapse. Thus the slouched curve of the back will be straightened.

A fun aid to create vertical poise
A useful idea to keep you upright without strain is to imagine that you have a ball of air between you and your horse. To help

you understand this concept more, stop reading and try this exercise. Put your hands out in front of you, palms facing inwards, shoulder-width apart. Imagine you are holding a big ball of air. Pat it with tiny movements. Do you notice a feeling of repelling magnets between your hands? Imagine your left hand is the horse's neck, and the right hand is your back. Keep that space between you and your horse by using this image. It's a fantastic reminder to keep you poised and in the movement without tension. Ask your friend for feedback to make sure you are not leaning forwards (putting the horse on the forehand) or backwards (sitting behind the movement and hollowing the horse's back), but are sitting in the vertical, with your head well poised on the top of your spine – 'on the bit'.

To correct **slouching** let the front of your body grow upwards and your back grow downwards; and to correct a **stiff upper body**, the opposite applies.

To stop your upper body from slouching, think of a ball of air between you and your horse. Honour that space between you. It will help keep him off his forehand too.

Rising trot

Rising trot is very challenging because to stay in the movement demands good balance, an open hip, the ability to lengthen down the back of the leg to the heel, and the front of your body to be open and leading.

For those of us living a sedentary life this is not so easy because we spend most of our time sitting, usually slouched. This has the effect of weakening and closing down the front of the body. Use the yoga exercise shown right to enliven and strengthen the muscles that have become weak.

First practise rising trot while stationary. Ask a friend to assist you. Use a neck strap on the horse to help you balance at first so that you don't fall backwards and bang down on the horse's back. Stand up in your stirrups and bring your knees back under your hips to balance yourself. You may be surprised

Use this dismounted exercise to help open the front of the body and your hips.

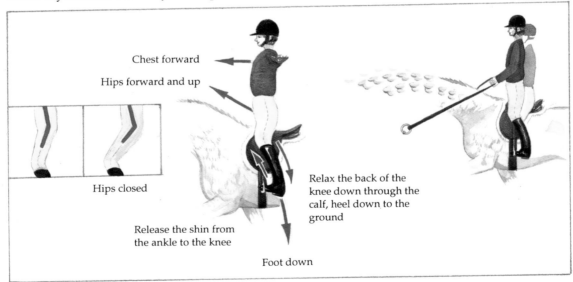

Exercise to open the angle of the hips in rising trot.

To avoid shortening the horse's neck, imagine his vertebrae floating away from you, as if you are at the base of a big wave.

how far back your lower leg and feet have to go in order to support your position. (As your suppleness and openness increase, your lower legs will come into a more conventional place.)

Now proceed in walk. Hold the neck strap and ask your friend to lead you. When you can balance in the movement practise a few strides of rising trot (whilst still walking). Let your body organise you and find that balancing point to help keep your hips open, knees down and lower leg back. Imagine you are kneeling on the ground as you rise. Let your knee slide down the saddle with each rise. As you rise allow your lower abdomen to move forwards and up, chest moving forwards. Allow yourself to lengthen from your pubic bone to your chin.

When you can rise and sit in walk, go forwards to trot. You may find you get left behind the movement at first, so use your neck strap. Only trot slowly and for a few strides. You may find your lower leg has crept forwards. If so, halt and repeat the exercises from the beginning. Use the ball of air idea as an extra aid to keep you open in front. As you rise, lead with your head and at the same time allow your feet to drop in the opposite direction, to the floor. Releasing more from the seat bone to the heel allows more length in the whole of the back of the leg, which brings the lower leg into the correct position. Be careful not to raise your chest unnaturally as this will hollow your lower back.

When you are more adept at rising trot, try this exercise: change the diagonal in the air, i.e. stand for two beats instead of one. If you are behind the movement you will fall back; if you are in front you will fall forwards. Practise until you can change the diagonal in the air and remain completely in balance.

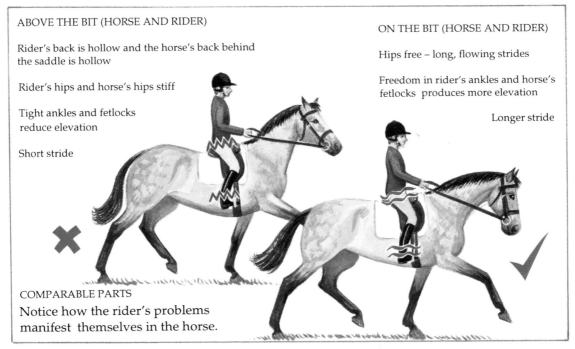

ABOVE THE BIT (HORSE AND RIDER)

Rider's back is hollow and the horse's back behind the saddle is hollow

Rider's hips and horse's hips stiff

Tight ankles and fetlocks reduce elevation

Short stride

ON THE BIT (HORSE AND RIDER)

Hips free – long, flowing strides

Freedom in rider's ankles and horse's fetlocks produces more elevation

Longer stride

COMPARABLE PARTS
Notice how the rider's problems manifest themselves in the horse.

Sitting trot

Unfortunately it is common to see sitting trot being practised endlessly, with horse and rider spending hours being lunged and both getting sorer and stiffer and the horse hollow and above the bit. This is not how it should be. If the horse is hollow it is inappropriate and damaging to continue in this way. Instead try to find out why he is hollowing. Perhaps you are restricting him, not allowing him the full use of his spine, or maybe he is upset about something. It could be that the saddle doesn't fit (too narrow is very common) or his back does not have the freedom to achieve the necessary tone and suppleness to raise up and support your weight.

Look at the illustrations opposite. Notice the different outline of the back and belly of the two horses. The first one's back is dropped (hollow). His abdominal muscles, being weak, have no tone (the same is true in humans). Now compare the second horse – his back is up and the abdominal muscles (belly) are working.

Practising sitting trot is pointless unless your horse is working as in the lower picture. Until then you need to rise to make it easy for the horse to bring his back up and strengthen it.

Notice also in the rounded horse (shown bottom right) the shape of space under his chin. This space is very important because the more the underside of his spine lengthens the more the topline can lengthen and raise up and the hindquarters engage, bringing more elevation and grace. When the correct outline is established, there is no resistance in the horse, school movements and transitions will engage the quarters more, transferring the weight back, and the forehand will lighten and lift.

HOLLOW

This horse has a weak and stiff back. Practising sitting trot on a horse in this condition/position can cause damage and has no purpose.

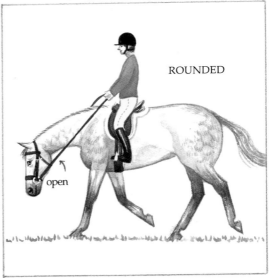

ROUNDED

open

This horse is working to stretch and strengthen his back. Note the back is raised, abdominal muscles are working and his nose is just in front of the vertical.

When practising sitting trot use the same body directions as described on page 13 and as illustrated below. Let your whole body be moved by the horse and receive as much upward support from him as the weight you release down onto him. Check the following:

- Is your head leading?
- Are you hips alive and moving with his back?
- Are you allowing your joints to open and absorb the movement?
- Are you using the ball of air to help support you?

Allow the weight of your hips and legs to fall down to the floor. Let your legs and hips belong to your horse and follow the movement of his ribcage, whilst from the waist up you allow your ribcage to open up – giving you, the rider, self-carriage.

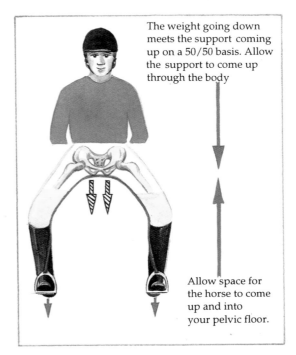

The weight going down meets the support coming up on a 50/50 basis. Allow the support to come up through the body

Allow space for the horse to come up and into your pelvic floor.

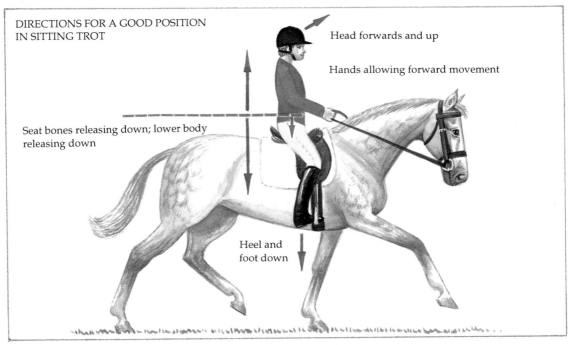

DIRECTIONS FOR A GOOD POSITION IN SITTING TROT

Head forwards and up

Hands allowing forward movement

Seat bones releasing down; lower body releasing down

Heel and foot down

Canter

The canter is a three-beat gait with a moment of suspension when all four feet are off the ground.

In the canter it is essential that you allow the horse to rock your pelvis forwards and backwards keeping your lower back and hips free. Allow your legs to hang down heavily to the ground. Your buttocks remain relaxed, knees and ankles elastic and ribcage floating.

As you can see in the illustration below, the rocking horse in canter, the horse's back slants downhill. This is when you must relax the front of your body and allow it to stretch like a rubber band – in fact, you give yourself to the horse. Use your ball of air for support. Allow your hip joints to open. Open your knee to allow the weight of your legs down to the floor, keeping you in the vertical and giving you the feeling of standing on the ground with a horse in between your legs.

You are now on the front rim of your seat bones.

Next the horse brings you up, onto the back rim, closing your hip joints. Let your seat bones open up sideways to make room for the horse's back to come up.

The horse's motion in canter should automatically close and open your hips and move your pelvis. All you have to do is allow it to happen. Feel the front, middle and back of the saddle. If you don't allow him to move you when his hind feet are coming under, you will block his movement and thus the engagement of his hindquarters.

Use the ball of air to give you more support, and breathe in through your nose when the horse is going down. When he is coming up, breathe out. **Remember that 50/50 relationship between the weight of your body and the support of his.** Sit and let the horse do the work.

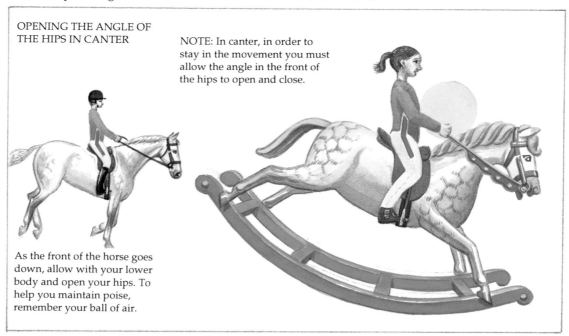

OPENING THE ANGLE OF THE HIPS IN CANTER

NOTE: In canter, in order to stay in the movement you must allow the angle in the front of the hips to open and close.

As the front of the horse goes down, allow with your lower body and open your hips. To help you maintain poise, remember your ball of air.

To help develop a long, effective leg in canter imagine your feet are broad and long – like ducks' web feet. Your toes are lengthening and widening; the whole of the soles of your feet spread down onto the stirrups, to the ground.

Stretching in canter on a long rein
Practice this exercise first on the left rein, in canter. Take your reins into your right hand. Put your left hand into the air, fingertips pointing to the sky. As you feel the horse fall away from you towards the ground, breathe in and hang from your fingertips, allowing your hip joints to open. Receive the upward support from the horse as you give your lower body to that support. Breathe out and keep hanging from your fingertips while you notice his body come back up to you; allow your hips joints to close. Now change hands. Repeat the exercise on the right rein.

To prevent gripping up, relax your knee and feel for the ground with your big webbed feet as the horse canters. This will make your legs longer and more effective.

CLOSING THE ANGLE OF
THE HIPS IN CANTER

As the horse comes up, his action will automatically close your hips – if you allow it to do so.

Final tips ■ ■ ■ ■ ■ ■ ■ ■ ■ ■ ■ ■ ■ ■

Using weight aids to solve problems on circles and turns

When a horse is balanced, his weight is distributed evenly over all four feet.

When the horse **falls in** on a turn or circle, the weight of his body is more over the inside legs. You can compare this to riding a bike. When you bank over on a bike, in order to straighten it you need to push on the outside pedal. Well, the same applies to your horse. If you push more on the outside stirrup as his ribcage swings to the inside, you will redistribute the weight onto all four feet again.

The opposite applies if the horse is **falling out**. In this case his weight is distributed more over the outside legs, so to bring him into balance push down more on the inside stirrup when his ribcage swings to the outside.

Conclusion

With this knowledge you can probably see now that previously you may have actively prevented your horse from using his body to its optimum and from going on the bit with ease and desire. Now you have acquired new skills from this book you can work in true partnership with your horse, both equally sharing the role of teacher and pupil.

Happy riding.

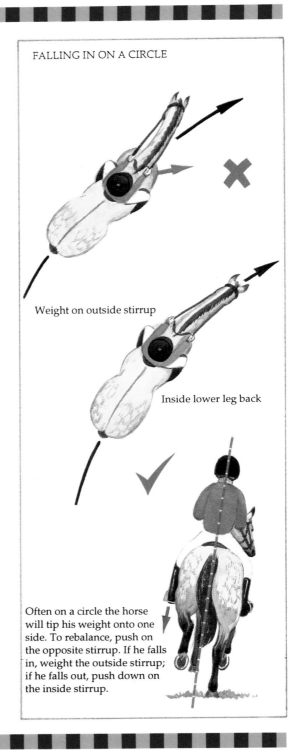

FALLING IN ON A CIRCLE

Weight on outside stirrup

Inside lower leg back

Often on a circle the horse will tip his weight onto one side. To rebalance, push on the opposite stirrup. If he falls in, weight the outside stirrup; if he falls out, push down on the inside stirrup.